A Guide to Making a Survival Fire

Table of Contents

A Guide to Making a Survival Fire 1

Introduction 3

Chapter 1: The Basics of a Survival Fire 5

Chapter 2: How to Make a Survival Fire 13

Chapter 3: Quick Tips to Make a Survival Fire
....20

Conclusion 39

Introduction

"The fire is the main comfort of the camp, whether in summer or winter, and is about as ample at one season as at another. It is as well for cheerfulness as for warmth and dryness."

- Henry David Thoreau

I want to thank you and congratulate you for purchasing the book "A Guide to Making a Survival Fire".

This book contains proven steps and strategies on how you to create a survival fire efficaciously.

Knowing how to start a fire is essentialespecially when you are trying to survive a wilderness or an emergency survival situation. Here's an inescapable fact: you will need to learn how to start a fire with or without any fire gear you are carrying. You need to learn to start a fire in the primitive ways. This book will help you survive any emergency situation, prepared or unprepared.

If you do not learn to create a survival fire, you will not be able to survive the night out in the wild. When you are caught in wilderness, there is a lot of things to be wary about after dark and fire will help you survive longer.

It's time for you to become an expert in.

Chapter 1: The Basics of a Survival Fire

"Next to knowing how to dress well, fire is one of the most important bush skills there are, because it is one of the few means available to make up most great deficiencies."

– Mors Kochanski

Fire is an essential source of life. Humans and animals cannot live without fire because it provides light, heat, and energy. Fire can be constructive and destructive depending on how you want to use it. Fire has been discovered and used since primitive time. It is indeed one of the best discoveries known to mankind.

If you want to survive in the wilderness or an emergency, it is essential that you know how to make a survival fire efficaciously. Prepare for a fire and making one is not difficult. All you need is patience and the rice equipment to help you start and maintain it.

Making fire to generate heat and light made it possible for our ancestors to cook food. The heat produced from a growing fire helped them stay warm in cold weather. Fire also kept predators away.

Even though there are more sophisticated ways to make fire today, but a wilderness emergency can catch us off-guard. You may or may not be prepared with a fire starter-kit. In such scenarios, it is best to get down to the basics as that is what helped our ancestors make fire instantly.

Knowing some basic fire-making techniques can increase your chances of survival in the wilderness. Building a fire requires three essential elements, i.e. heat, oxygen and fuel. Only when these 3 elements are present together, a fire can burn easily. Remove one of these elements and the fire will cease to burn.

- **Heat** – The heat source is essential for the initial starting of the fire. This heat is caused by high temperature that you can trap from the sun's rays or a friction between 2 stones. This heat is even required to maintain and grow the fire. The heat allows this fire to spread by warming surrounding air, removing the moisture from nearby fuel, and preheating the fuel in its path. This, in turn, enables the fire to grow with greater ease.

- **Oxygen** – Oxygen is abundantly found all around us. About 21% of the air we breathe contains oxygen. Most fires require about 16% oxygen to burn successfully. Oxygen acts as an oxidizing agent supporting the very chemical process that occurs inside a fire.

- **Fuel** – Fuel can be any combustible material that helps a fire burn. It can be in the form of solid, liquid or gas. Combustible materials can be lit from clothes, twigs, branches, wood shavings, dried leaves, cotton, charred cloth, etc. that are usually fed as fuel to the fire. The level of moisture in the material is the determining factor on how well that fuel will burn. Anything with low moisture content is a better combustible material.

When a combustible material is exposed to high temperature or heat due to friction or a spark, it quickly ignites and catches fire. It is not possible to use a match on a log to start a fire. You need to start from the scratch in order to successfully start a fire. Make sure you have plenty of tinder and kindling materials to sustain the fire before permitting it to grow.

Benefits of Fire

Starting a fire will provide you the following benefits:

- **Warmth**: Fire can keep you warm even in the cold weather or snow. The fire, along with some clothes, should help you survive the long dark nights, until you find some rescue.

- **Light to see**: Fire can enable you see even in dark. This becomes very important especially when you are trapped in the wilderness. You would always want to keep an eye on what lurks behind the tree or bush.

- **Keeps nocturnal predators away**: Fire is an important weapon after dark to keep predators away. When wild beasts see fire near a camp, they tend to stay away because they are scared of the fire.

- **Cooks food**: You can use this fire to cook raw meat or canned food, to make sure what you are eating is healthy. Fire removes bacteria at high temperatures so cook your raw food before you eat. You will not want to fall sick when you are the middle of a forest.

- **Purifies water**: A strong and growing fire can help you boil water and keep it ready in case you are thirsty. You can avoid dehydration even amidst sheer wilderness.

- **Keeps insects and bugs away**: Fire wards off those insidious and irritating insects bugs and pests we all hate to encounter. You may require additional assistance, such as insect repellants, mosquito net, elevated bedding, and other defense weapons to help you further.

- **Feels good**: A growing and strong fire can make you feel good. It is a mood-lifter and you will feel the positive benefits once it is lit. You will feel safe, secure and not suicidal.

- **Disinfects wounds**: Though this is not recommended without proper training or practice, fire is a good way to sterilize tools or disinfect wounds such as, cuts and open injuries. You can avoid preliminary infection doing this but you will require immediate help to prevent worsening scenarios.

- **Signals for distress calls**: Building a fire is a great way to get noticed in case you are waiting for rescue. When people see smoke or fire, they may come looking for you.

When you start a fire make sure you build a ring of safety around the fire to avoid fire hazards. Keep your ring wide, about 10 inches diameter, to ensure that any sparks or falling debris don't ignite the rest of the area. Avoid building campfires under hanging branches. Keep water nearby in case you need to extinguish an out-of-control fire. Keep a shovel ready in case you have to smother an out-of-control fire with dirt. Do not leave a campfire unattended. Keep the fire as small as you need it. Remember, in order to stop a fire, take out of the elements of the fire triangle completely, i.e. heat, fuel, and oxygen.

If you are able to start a fire successfully, you will understand the true benefits of this magnanimous source of energy. Don't misuse or mistreat it as it can bring disaster. Use it to help you save your life and get out of your emergency as soon as possible.

Chapter 2: How to Make a Survival Fire

If you are a nature lover and love trekking into the wilderness, you will unanimously need to learn how to make a survival fire.

If you are stuck in a forest, you will have ample wood at your disposal. In a survival situation, fire has 3 essential roles to play:
- Cooking
- Signaling
- Providing warmth.

Different kinds of wood can be used to start a fire. They are mainly:
- **Tinder**–this comprises the dry and fluffy wood shavings, dry leaves, straw, fine sawdust, scraps of bamboo, charred cloth pieces, down feathers of birds, dry lichens, cedar barks, lint from old clothes or a pair of jeans, hay, gun

powder, dead evergreen needles, waxed paper, dried vegetable fibers, etc.

- **Kindling** – this comprises the small twigs and splinters of wood, pieces of heavy cardboard, strips of tree barks, small pieces of wood, wood that has been in close contact with highly flammable sources such as, kerosene, any oil, gasoline, etc.

- **Fuel wood**–this comprises the larger logs or combustible materials that can grow and maintain the fire, such as dry standing tree logs, dead branches, twisted bunch of dry green grass, finely split green wood, oil, charcoal, dried animal dung, animal fats, etc. Fuel wood forms the backbone of the fire. The size and the type of logs used can play a crucial role in determining the duration of the fire. The longer or heavier the logs and branches are, the longer will be the duration of the fire. Hardwood is the best type of wood used for fueling a fire.

Depending on the densities of the wood, we can differentiate it as a hardwood or softwood. In North Carolina, you can use Mullein, Cedar, Cotton Wood (Poplar), etc. as softwood. If you want dry wood, you can take wood from a fallen or dead tree. Make sure the wood doesn't crumble when you drill or spin it. It is all part of a learning experience.

<u>Prepare for the Fire</u>

You need to first gather wood for the fire. You need to have enough tinder, kindling, and fuel wood to last the fire for a while. The wood cannot be wet. Avoid using green leaves or twigs, as it will not catch fire easily. Before you lay the wood for fire, make sure you check the wood. If the wood snaps easily, then it can be used for fire. Anything else should be discarded. You can also use lint from your jeans or pockets to use as tinder. You can also use small scraps of paper, Q-tips from cotton buds, the fluff from wool clothing, deodorant sticks, hand sanitizer, petroleum jelly, insect repellent, etc. to ignite a fire.

Build the Fire Ring

Now build the fire ring by clearing the ground in a large circle away from the trees. The circle should be at least 2 meter away from any tree. Make a barrier of big rocks to demarcate the flammable area from the rest of the forest. This barrier will help contain and maintain the fire for a longer duration. Once the fire is contained, you can use it to cook food, boil water and keep you warm. Keep the barrier wide open, as fire needs plenty of oxygen to keep burning. The barrier will help contain the fire even when there are strong gusts of breeze around. Now place a big pile of tinder in the center to help ignite a fire. Add a small amount of kindling on top to keep the flame rising once the tinder catches fire. You can also add some fuel, if available, on the tinder.

Create the Ember

You can create an ember using any fire-making methods, such as using 2 stones to strike each other, flint and steel, bow drill, fire piston, reflectors, etc. Depending on the equipment you have, which time of the day you want to make the fire, your stamina and physical strength, and the current weather condition, you can use any of the proven fire-making methods.

Start the Fire

Once you have the set-up ready, it is time to make the survival fire. Use your device or method to light the tinder. As soon as you see your tinder smolder, start blowing into it continuously till you see a flame. Make sure you don't blow very hard, else the flame will die. Fire will start consuming the tinder and the fuel quickly. Add more fuel and kindling to help the fire burn easily. Add fuel wood to the fire every few hours to keep the fire burning through the day or night. Make sure you have plenty of fuel wood stacked up nearby so that you don't have to find more in the darkness or if your fire is about to go out. In case you have wet wood, you can place them around the ring to help dry them. The more the fuel, the bigger the fire will grow. Depending on your need or necessity, you can build a bigger fire. If you don't want to attract much attention, you can keep the fire low.

If you want to cook, you can create a tripod with wood and hang a pot or raw meat to cook in the fire. If you want to signal with the fire, you can add a living branch of wet leaves to the fire to produce a large cloud of smoke. Make sure that the fire is strong and self-sustaining before you attempt to do this, so it is not extinguished. You can also light a branch with leaves with this fire and signal in Morse code to signal for help.

The fire can also help keep you warm when there is snow. You can dry all your clothes before the fire. Just make sure it is not very close, as to catch fire.

No one wants to be in an emergency where they have to wait for help. It is indeed scary. But it is always better to be safe than sorry. When you know the best ways to survive an emergency, you are prepared for the worst, even in wilderness.

Chapter 3: Quick Tips to Make a Survival Fire

When you find yourself in an emergency or wilderness survival situation, it is essential to know how to start a fire. It will not only help you survive the night from cold and predators, but also it will provide light to you and help you cook food. When you are out camping, make sure you carry a fire starting gear always. If not, then you will have to start your own fire in the primitive ways.

Make sure you learn as many fire-starting methods as possible before you head out alone into the wilderness. You need to start with building your fire correctly so that when you light the fire, it stays lit for a long time.

Fire is an essential element of our lives. When you are in a survival situation, starting a fire can mean the difference between life and death. Maybe you always carry a fire-starting gear. Consider it lost, wet or just used up. What then? Are you self-sufficient to start your own fire then? Fire offers us protection, heat, platform to cook food, light, heat or purify water, signal for help, etc. We take it for granted in our natural surroundings but when we are out in the wild, nothing comes for free. You have to work hard to make it happen, all alone. So be prepared and be strong!

Let us look at the different ways to start a fire:

- **Flint and steel** – This is one of the easiest primitive ways to start a fire. All you need is a flint and a piece of carbon steel (such as, survival knife). You can light a survival fire with flint and survival knife in any condition. You need to start by striking the flint against the knife and create a friction between them. The friction created between the two will generate sparks in no time.

The surface needs to get heated so use some force. Keep some tinder ready for you to ignite as soon as the sparks start emitting. Now gently blow the sparks towards the tinder to start the fire burning. This primitive way of starting fire is relatively easy, even for a kid. You need the least physical stamina and only two items to start the fire. You can try the same with 2 stones. It works the same way and another alternative in case you don't have your survival knife kit either.

- **Bow Drill**–This may seem a bit more complicated than the above-mentioned methods. Once again, you need to find a hardwood or a rock or anything hard with a groove or an abscess inside. This is basically the socket that the drill will fit into. Now find another stick that can serve as a drill. The equipment is easy to make and you will notice that it is relatively uncomplicated in terms of construction. The drill needs to be about three-fourth inch thick. With your knife carve the end of this stick to make a rounded point.

The fireboard should be at least 1 inch thick. Drill a tiny groove into it 1-inch diameter, for the drill to rest in. Now, cutout a triangle shaped notch that will connect the hole to the board's side. Find a bendable stick to make a bow. Tie a string or cord to both the ends of this bow. Place the tinder into this triangular notch in the fireboard.

Note that this is where you will see the fire when it is ignited. Although a bow drill is more difficult to build, it sure is the faster way to create fire and with less effort. Keep the fireboard firmly in place with your foot. Place the bowstring around the drill. Place the rounded point of the drill into the groove in the fireboard. Now continuously pull the bow back and forth until there is enough friction and heat to ignite the sparks. Gently blow to catalyze the fire formation.

- **Hand Drill**–You need a drill and a fireboard you create this bush craft technique of making fore. It requires more physical strength, patience and skill to construct and implement this technique. Instead of the bow, two hands are needed to spin the drill. This creates enough friction and heat to create sparks. To create this drill, find a softwood stick and chisel one end to make a rounded tip. You can use your survival knife to do this. Now cut a small hole in the fireboard just about an inch from the edge of the fireboard. Now cut a v-shaped notch that connects the hole and the edge of the fireboard.

The point of the v should connect to the hole. Evenly distribute tinder throughout the v-shaped notch on the fireboard. Now hold the drill firmly with both palms of your hands and with great force start spinning the drill into the hole of the fireboard. Apply downward pressure. Keep spinning the drill until you see sparks emerge and then gently keep blowing till the tinder catches the flame.

- **Pump Drill**–The pump drill is the most difficult to build. But once it is constructed, it takes almost no time to make the fire. A pump drill is just like a bow drill, but operated in a different manner. Just like a bow drill, it also uses a drill and a fireboard. The main difference is how the drill is rotated here. A pump drill essentially works by pumping the drill up and down.
Now let us see how to construct a pump drill. First and foremost, find a round piece of hardwood to serve as the drill. Now cut a small hole in the center.

Using some type of cord, attach a sharp rock to the end of this hardwood stick. Next, drill a hole through a rock with the same width of this hardwood stick. Push the stick through the hole. The rock should not move. Find another piece of hardwood and drill a hole through the center. It should be of the same width as the drill. Insert this piece of hardwood onto the drill, an inch above the rock. Make sure that the bow in the wood is facing upward.

Make two holes on the ends of each side of this bow so that a string can be tied around easily to form the bow. Make sure that the arrow is resting about one to two inches above the rock. Now connect both the sides of this bow to the end of the drill with a cord. It should be in the direction away from the arrow. Use another hardwood to create the fireboard with the groove to hold the tinder. Grab the bow of the drill and point it towards the groove of the fireboard. Now spin the device upwards. When it unwinds, the drill is driven into the fireboard and sparks emerge. This technique is effortless in the creation of fire as long as you can master the art of constructing the device.

- **Fire Piston**–This is a rather unique method of making fire that relies completely on air heating up under compression. It may be a bit more complicated to build, as it requires more technology. It is still considered as primitive technique of making fire. It uses the technique of creating pressure while plunging down the piston to generate enough heat to create sparks. Let us now create a fire piston.

First, you will need a strong plastic or copper pipe about 10 cm long. Make the ends smooth. Now plug one end of the pipe using a piece of metal, brass cap or wood. Make sure it fits well into the hole of the pipe. Now take a thick wooden plunger slightly narrower than the pipe, so that it can fit into the pipe. Cut it so that it is a couple of centimeters longer than the pipe. Insert the plunger into the pipe to make sure it moves up and down without much issue. Note, a fire piston consists of a cylinder (a plastic pipe) and a plunger that fits into this cylinder with a nearly air-tight seal.

Now, insert a 10-millimeter rubber ring around the ring of the piston. This side will enter the copper pipe or cylinder. Lubricate the rubber ring. Stash some char cloth or tinder inside the cylinder. Now with great force and speed, push the piston into the tube quickly and pull it back out immediately. Continue until you see sparks forming and igniting the tinder inside the cylinder. Building a fire piston may take some time and effort, but it is an effortless way to create a survival fire. It is light weight and compact.

- **Fire Plough** – This is one of the simplest ways of making a fire using native materials. Rubbing two sticks of wood together creates this fire. This technique is used on the Pacific islands. Start by finding a flat piece of native wood for the baseboard. It should be couple of inches thick. Cut a straight line down the center on the flat side. You can use your survival knife to finish this task. Now simply hollow out this line to create a shallow and thin abscess about one-fourth inch wide. Now time to make the plough!

Find a softwood stick that is at least 1-inch thick. Now use your knife to carve the end of this softwood stick to make a rounded point. The tip should be small enough to fit into the groove on the baseboard. Now rub the two crafted parts together. This should create sufficient friction that will generate required heat to initiate a fire. You need to keep up the continual force. Keep rubbing the softwood stick through the groove in the baseboard, starting at one end and going toward the other. You need to use a lot of force for this task.

As you keep doing this, you will notice that wood starts to shave off. This continuous friction will create sufficient heat that will ignite the wood shavings. Once your kindling is ready, just gently start blowing onto the sparks inside the tinder in order to start a flame. This primitive fire making technique can be used in any condition, in any location, though it requires a lot of physical strength and stamina to get this working.

Other fire-making strategies that can help you in complete wilderness are:

- **Reflectors**–Even something as insignificant as a flashlight reflector can help you to make a survival fire. When there is sunlight, you can use a reflector to ignite a piece of highly flammable tinder by placing it exactly where the bulb is usually located. All you need to do is, just focus towards the direction of the sun. This will create enough heat to ignite the tinder. Reflectors work by concentrating the sun's rays to a point. Typically any parabolic reflector can do this job. Common examples of parabolic reflectors are, reflector in a flashlight, the polished bottom of a soda can, reflector in a car headlight, a stainless steel bowl, a satellite antenna with a shiny, polished surface, etc.

- **Lenses**–As with reflectors, you can also make fire with any lens or magnifiers. All you need is convex lens. Some common lenses that you can typically use are, the convex side of Eyeglasses (far-sighted eyeglass), Camera lens, Magnifying glass, a clear plastic or glass bottle filled with water, Fresnel lens, transparent light bulb, binoculars, etc. You can use any magnifying lens on a sunny day to light a fire. In fact, a drop of water on the glass can intensify the sunlight. If you are a wildlife admirer, make sure to pack a pocket magnifier that is about one and a half inches in diameter. It can come handy to create a survival fire. Simply hold the lens at an angle such that the sun's light is focused into the smallest concentrated area possible. Try to angle the lens so that the bright dot is as small as possible. Now, place some tinder under this concentrated spot watch it start to smoke soon. Blow gently to generate a flame.

Binoculars can also make a great magnifier. If you are carrying a binocular, just turn them around and use the lens you keep your eyes on, to focus the sunlight onto the tinder. Note the smallest brightest light. Now your tinder will smolder any moment. Have you ever tried to light fire using a broken, transparent light bulb. Use the broken inside of the bulb and add some water to the cavity of the bulb. This will act as an instant lens to focus sunlight.

You can also create fire from water. All you need is a small, transparent plastic bag filled with water. Now tie the plastic bag and hold it such that the plastic bag forms a sphere. You will actually create a makeshift lens in this way. Now place some tinder under this sphere and focus the sphere onto the tinder until you notice the small, brightened spot. Slowly you will notice the ember. Is this not easy and handy? All you need is sun, water and a transparent plastic bag.

Not surprised yet? You can even make a fire out of ice. Just find a frozen stream or pond. Now, cut a piece of clear piece of ice out of it. Make sure that the ice is as transparent and clear as possible. Use your survival knife to saw and create the required shape for block of the ice in order to make the 2 opposite sides of it convex. Now using your hands smoothen the 2 convex sides and finishing the lens. Rest is the usual process of focusing the ice lens to ignite the fire. One way to get clear ice involves making a hole in pre-existing lake ice. This creates a freezing environment for clear ice. Since, the cold temperature is applied from only one side, the impurities are pushed down into the lake water and carried away. So you will be left with clear ice on top.

- **Fire from Can and Chocolate bar–** The 2 favorite snacks, chocolate and Coke. You can create fire using just these

2 items. The bottom of a Coke or any other can is ideal for concentrating and focusing the sun's light. It is although a bit dull and not shiny enough to focus the sun's rays to ignite tinder. You can use just a piece of the chocolate bar to polish up the bottom of this can. Try to use pure chocolate only. Once you have finished polishing the bottom of the can, you will see a huge difference. It will have a mirror-like effect.

If you don't have chocolate, you can also use toothpaste for the polishing. Now use the bottom of the can to reflect the sun's rays to ignite fire. Typically, you can hold the tinder at the focal point of the bottom, about one to 1.25 inches away from the center of the bottom. Make sure you orient the bottom of the can towards the sun. The easiest way to find the focal point is by adjusting a sheet of paper till you see the smallest, bright spot. This is where you should hold the tinder.

- **Batteries**–You can also use batteries to start a fire. You need batteries and a conductor to start this fire. Typically you can use steel wool or gum wrappers as conductors. Just bridge the 2 battery terminals with the steel wool and you will instantly notice a spark of fire. You can lead the steel wool to the tinder bundle that is eventually going to burn. You can use 9-volt battery, or two AA or AAA batteries for this task. You can also start a fire with one AA or AAA battery but this may take a little bit longer to ignite.

You can also start a fire using car batteries. You can connect the jumper cable with both the car's battery terminals (positive as well as negative) and then briefly make the jumper cables touch together. Now you will see immediately create hot sparks that can be used to make a survival fire.

- **Other Fire-making methods**–There are other ways of starting a fire. You can use a coffee tin and stash a cotton rag into it. Now use a fair quantity of linseed oil to moisten the cloth. You can use a digital multimeter to monitor temperature. After a decent amount of time, and good supply of oxygen or air, you will notice spontaneous combustion of the rag.

You can also use wine glasses oriented in the wrong direction to help focus the sun's rays onto the tinder. Kitchen measuring cups or spoons, soup ladles, etc. made of stainless steel are excellent reflectors.

You can also buy magnesium starter kits from any outdoor store. The magnesium burns well when it is shaven into fine filings. Gather the filings into a small pile and use the backside of your knife blade to create spark from ferrocerium rod on this pile of magnesium filings. You can even put the same pile of these magnesium filings on a bundle of tinder so that it can readily catch fire.

You should try to learn and practice as many fire-making methods as possible. You can land in an emergency anywhere and you never know what your situation will be like. By being able to make a survival fire quickly and effectively in any weather conditions, you will be better prepared for any emergency situations. These fire-making techniques should help you in most of the situations.

Conclusion

Thank you again for purchasing this book!

I truly hope this book helped you understand how to make a survival fire quick and efficiently.

Your next step is to practice the different fire-making methods near your house or outside your house to make sure you are adept at adapting quick even when there is a wilderness emergency.

Thank you and good luck!

Printed in Poland
by Amazon Fulfillment
Poland Sp. z o.o., Wrocław

Animal Mysteries

Contents

Follow Those Tracks! — 2

Mystery on Hayden Peak — 8

The Animal Files — 18

Animal Detectives — 26

Follow Those Tracks!

Written by Patricia J. Murphy

Psst... hey you!

Do you want to solve a mystery? How about an animal mystery? Yes, *you* can uncover lots of animal mysteries. That is, you can if you know where to look. If you look in the right way at the right moment, you may get a glimpse of something REALLY wild!

Animal tracking or nature tracking is like detective work. It lets us sneak a peek into the lives of wild animals. Anyone can do it. Why not give it a try?

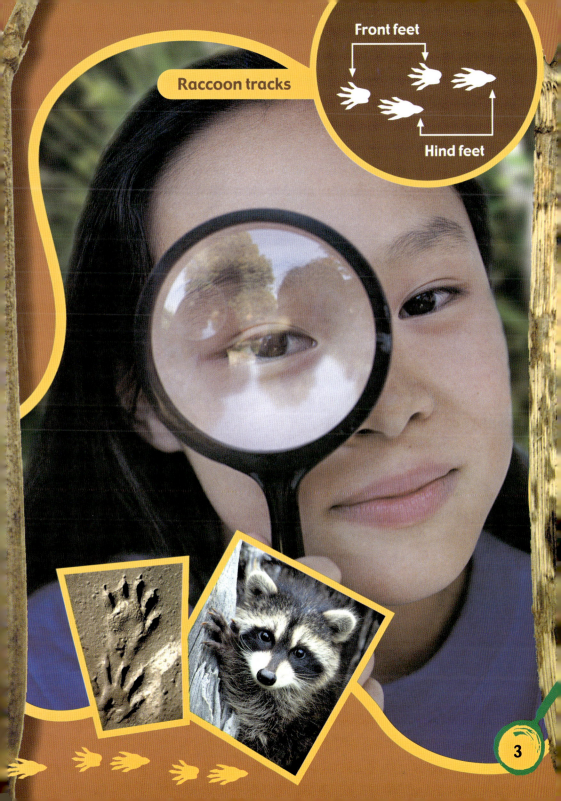

Raccoon tracks

Front feet

Hind feet

Tracking Tips

Grab a backpack and some waterproof clothes. Then follow these tracking tips on your tracking trip!

Space Out

Choose open spaces, such as woods and parks, where you think animals are or perhaps were. Animal tracks are best seen in the mud, in soft ground, or right after a fresh snowfall.

Goose track

Be Careful

Know where you're going and where you've been. Bring an adult along. This will keep *you* from becoming a mystery!

Use Your Senses

Look, listen, touch, and smell as you hunt for clues. Look for tracks, teeth marks, and tail trails. Hunt for animal droppings, homes, nests, and holes, but don't disturb them. Listen for sounds. Note any smells.

Goose nest

Study the Clues

It's time to solve the mystery! Tracking tools will come in handy. Study the tracks. Examine any other clues. Photograph or sketch what you've found.

Tracking Tools

Squirrel

If you are tracking at dusk, dawn, or during the evening, put red cellophane over a torch. The animals can't see the red light, but you can see them!

Nature Guide

"Remember to use your common sense," says Brian Winters, an animal-tracking expert. "Think about what kinds of animals live nearby—such as a neighbourhood dog or the crow that's cawing overhead. You may not be able to make a positive identification, but you will get close."

These hints will help you get closer to solving an animal mystery:

Look at the size of the track, the shape, and the number of toes and claws. Then look in a nature guide to see what kind of track it might be.

Measure the distance between the tracks. This can tell you how fast or slow the animal was moving.

Follow the tracks. The tracks may show you where the animal went. They might also uncover an event, such as a fox chasing a rabbit!

So what are you waiting for? Tracking is a good way to connect with wild animals outside a zoo. "It teaches us that we share space with these animals," says Winters. "It teaches us respect for them and for their habitats." And that's no mystery at all!

Mystery on Hayden Peak

Written by Maggie Bridger
Photographed by Andy and Angie Belcher

My cousin Hal told me there were bears nearby. I looked at the tent we were putting up, made out of nylon as thin as tissue paper. A bear could rip it apart with a swipe of its claws. "Are there really bears here?" I asked.

"Sure," said Hal. "But nothing like the ferocious grizzly bears I've encountered in my mountain adventures. Once when I was climbing, I saw this grizzly–"

"We only have black bears up here–right, Dad?" said Liz, interrupting Hal. Liz is my other cousin. She and her dad, my uncle Ron, had invited Hal and me on this mountain-climbing trip.

"Right," replied Uncle Ron. "Black bears aren't as dangerous as grizzlies, but they certainly make a mess."

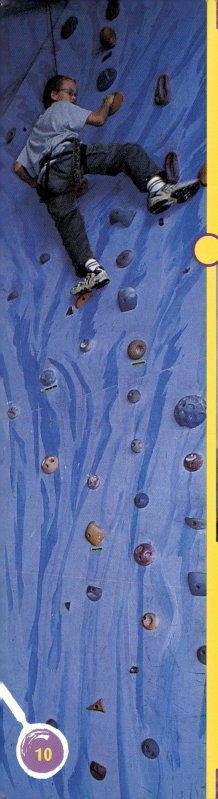

I tried not to show it, but I was really nervous about this adventure. It was OK for both Uncle Ron and Liz. They were mountain guides who had been to these mountains hundreds of times. Every summer, they used pack goats to carry food and supplies into the mountains.

It was OK for Hal, who was full of stories about all the mountain-climbing adventures he'd had. But I'm from the city, and I've never been camping before. I know a lot about rock climbing, but the only climbing I've done was at a rock gym. I was sure I was going to wreck this trip for everyone.

We arrived at camp in the middle of the day, and we were going to start our climb before dawn the next morning. "I need to explore possible routes to the mountain," said Uncle Ron.

"While you do that, could I practise climbing?" I asked. With more experience, I might not spoil the trip.

"I'll climb with you," said Liz. "Let me tie the goats up first so they won't follow us."

While Liz tied the goats and Uncle Ron and Hal got some rope to hang the food out of the bears' reach, I unpacked my backpack and organized all my stuff. As I was pulling things out of my pack, I put my tube of toothpaste on the rock next to my helmet.

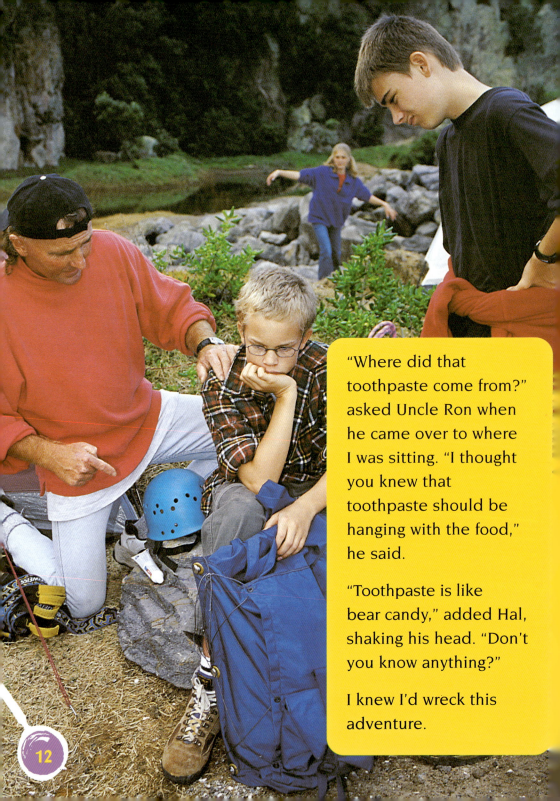

"Where did that toothpaste come from?" asked Uncle Ron when he came over to where I was sitting. "I thought you knew that toothpaste should be hanging with the food," he said.

"Toothpaste is like bear candy," added Hal, shaking his head. "Don't you know anything?"

I knew I'd wreck this adventure.

Just then, Liz came over, too. "Are you ready?" she asked. "We'd better get going so that we'll have plenty of time to practise climbing before the sun sets." I grabbed my climbing gear, and off we went.

I was halfway up the cliff when I remembered the toothpaste. I'd forgotten to put it back in my pack, and it was still on the rock. Bear candy!

When I told Liz, she cried, "If a bear finds the goats, it could attack them, and Hal and Dad are away from camp. We'd better get back down there. Come on!"

We raced back to camp expecting the worst and, when we got there, that's just what we found. One tent had collapsed and another was missing altogether!

"I've got to go and check on the goats!" shouted Liz.

"What happened?" asked Hal. He had just arrived in camp.

"A bear has been scavenging in our camp!"

We checked the site of the missing tent but could see no shredded nylon or bear tracks or any mess at all. I ran over to the rock where I'd left the toothpaste, but the tube hadn't been touched. "I thought bears liked toothpaste," I said. Hal shrugged.

Then I hurried over to find Liz. "The goats aren't the least bit upset," Liz told me. I could see their tracks showed no sign of panic. Something strange was going on.

When Liz and I got back from the goats, Uncle Ron was back. He shook his head when he saw the missing tent. "Your parents won't like this one bit," he said. "I hate to say this, but I think maybe we should cut our trip short."

Hal was reading *Mountain Adventures*. He didn't even look up.

All of a sudden, I had an idea of where I might find our tent–and the bear. "Come on, Hal," I said. "Let's search for the tent. Maybe the bear didn't drag it very far."

As soon as we were away from camp, I said, "Were *you* the bear, Hal?"

Hal headed for a pile of boulders and pulled out the tent. "I'm sorry. I didn't really want to ruin the trip for everyone. It's just that I've read a lot about climbing and practised in a gym," he said. "But the truth is I've never been in the mountains before. It's scarier than I thought."

"You know a lot about climbing," I said, "but you've been telling other people's stories. Don't you want to tell your own? Uncle Ron and Liz are experts. We'll be fine."

And we were. Hal was the first to the top of the mountain, but I was right behind him. Any bear in the area must have heard our whoops and hollers from the summit!

What clues made it clear that Hal was the "bear"?

The Animal Files

Written by Lisa Trumbauer

When is buying a souvenir a crime? When it's made from an endangered species! Proving something was made from an endangered animal can be hard. That's where the Wildlife Forensics Laboratory steps in.

Animal products from around the world are sent to the lab. There, scientists determine whether the body parts belong to endangered animals. They also try to find out how the animals were killed. They look at parts through microscopes. They analyze blood and tissue. And they run chemical tests. In many ways, the lab is like any other crime lab. And the case files are full of animal mysteries.

Confiscated skins

Live turtles and masks made from turtle shells

It is illegal in many countries to buy, sell, or import products made from endangered animals. Over 100 countries belong to a special group, called CITES, that monitors the trade in endangered animals.

File Name: The Case of the Aching Back
Endangered Animal: Bengal Tiger
Suspected Product: Medicine

TIGER

It was a tough case. But not an unusual one. It all started because of an aching back. A man bought some medicine in a shop. The shop sold traditional Chinese medicines. The words on the bottle's label stuck out: *Os tigris*. Could this mean "tiger bones"? The man sent the bottle to the Wildlife Forensics Lab for closer examination. Sure enough, tests showed tiger bones.

China has traditionally used tiger parts, such as bones and blood, in medicine. It is a crime in many countries to import medicines containing tiger parts. Shop owners in these countries need to beware. Like this shop owner, they can face stiff penalties if they are caught!

File Name: The Case of the Clever Carving
Endangered Animal: Elephant
Suspected Product: Statue Carving

ELEPHANT

After receiving a call from a concerned citizen, agents visited a gallery selling ivory statues. The art dealers said the ivory was from already extinct mastodons and woolly mammoths. It might have been possible. Ivory tusks from these animals have been found. However, the agents suspected that the statue was made of elephant ivory. The carvings were sent to the Wildlife Forensics team. Sure enough, extensive testing showed it was elephant ivory!

Most ivory comes from elephant tusks. To get the tusks, people kill the elephants. It's hard to imagine the world without elephants. It's even harder to imagine that someone would kill such a large animal for such a small prize.

File Name: The Case of the Suckered Surfers
Endangered Animal: Green Sea Turtle
Suspected Product: Guitar

TURTLE

This case had "sucker the tourist" written all over it. A group of surfers were returning from a Pacific island. All they bought was a guitar. That's all it took! The guitar was made from a sea turtle shell. Sea turtles are endangered. Products made from them are illegal in many countries.

People kill sea turtles for food and their shells. The shells can be made into items such as guitars. They can also be boiled into a glue-like substance and sold as turtle jelly. Possessing sea turtle items is a crime. The fines cost these surfers a lot more than the guitar!

Animal Detectives

Written by Lee Martin

Have you ever heard tales of Bigfoot? Have you ever wondered who searches for creatures like this? They are called cryptozoologists (*krip toh zoo AHL uh jists*). But not all animals they look for are as strange as Bigfoot.

Mountain gorilla

Cryptozoologists have found many once unknown animals that are well known today. Mountain gorillas were found in 1902. The Komodo dragon was found in 1912.

Komodo dragon

How do scientists find these mystery animals? I e-mailed expert Loren Coleman to find out...

Cryptozoology is the science of "hidden" or undiscovered animals.

E-mail interview

From: Lee Martin
To: Loren Coleman
Subject: E-mail interview

Loren Coleman

> How do cryptozoologists begin a search?

First you might talk to people who live in the area. Then you would actually search for the animals. You hope to photograph or capture and release them.

27

E-mail interview

> What new animals have been found?

New dolphins, whales, and fish are being discovered all the time. In March 2000, a crocodile thought to be extinct was found. In October 2000, another group of coelacanth (*COHL uh canth*) was found. This is a kind of fish. Many people thought it had been extinct for 65 million years. It was first "discovered" in 1938. In 2000, there were also new reports of Bigfoot sightings. An imprint of what might be a Bigfoot body was found in the mud.

Many mystery animals aren't mysteries to the people who live nearby. Often they are well known to people who live in the area before they are discovered by the rest of the world.

There have been many alleged Bigfoot sightings over the years. This shot (left) was taken in 1967 in northern California with a movie camera.

Do you believe in Bigfoot? Why or why not?

This cast of a footprint was made after the alleged sighting of Bigfoot in northern California in 1967.

E-mail interview

> Where in the world might new animals be discovered?

In 1992, a new kind of ox was located in the Vu Quang Nature Reserve in Vietnam. Many new mammals have been found in this jungle area of Vietnam. It is also known as the Lost World. Sumatra, the sixth largest island in the world, is a great place to find new animals, too. However, the world's oceans may hold the biggest surprises.

The Lost World

Vietnam

South-east Asia

Vu Quang ox

E-mail interview

> How do you prepare to be a cryptozoologist?

In most places, you can't study the subject in school. But you can do it on your own. Pick something that you are very interested in (for example, primates, giant squid, fossil men, and so on). Learn all about that topic. You can pursue this interest along with your other learning.

Index

bears	9, 11–14, 16–17
Bigfoot	26, 28–29
CITES	19
climbing	9–11, 13, 16–17
clues	4, 17
crime	18, 20, 24
cryptozoologists	26–27, 31
endangered animals	18–20, 22, 24
elephants	22
leopards	19
sea turtles	19, 24
tigers	20
goats	10–11, 13, 14–15
guitars	24
ivory	22
Komodo dragon	26
Lost World	30

mountain gorillas	26
souvenirs	18
statues	22
Sumatra	30
toothpaste	11–14
torch	5
tracking tips	4
tracking tools	4–5
tracks	2–7, 14, 15
dog	7
goose	4, 7
gull	7
rabbit	6, 7
raccoon	3, 7
turtle jelly	24
tusks	22
Vietnam	30
Vu Quang Nature Reserve	30
Wildlife Forensics Laboratory	18, 20, 22